MONSTERS & MYTHS
BLOODSUCKING BEASTS

By Lisa Regan

Gareth Stevens
Publishing

Please visit our Web site, www.garethstevens.com. For a free color catalog of all our high-quality books, call toll free 1-800-542-2595 or fax 1-877-542-2596.

Library of Congress Cataloging-in-Publication Data

Regan, Lisa.
 Bloodsucking beasts / Lisa Regan.
   p. cm. — (Monsters & myths)
 Includes index.
 ISBN 978-1-4339-4991-3 (library binding)
 ISBN 978-1-4339-4992-0 (pbk.)
 ISBN 978-1-4339-4993-7 (6-pack)
1. Vampires. 2. Bloodsucking animals. 3. Monsters. I. Title.
 GR830.V3R44 2011
 398'.4–dc22
                                    2010033444

Published in 2011 by
Gareth Stevens Publishing
111 East 14th Street, Suite 349
New York, NY 10003

Printed in the United States of America

CPSIA compliance information: Batch #CW11GS: For further information contact Gareth Stevens, New York, New York at 1-800-542-2595.

Table of Contents

Asanbosam

TAIL
Some stories say that the vampire has a long tail that ends in the head of a snake. It coils its tail around the branches of trees.

TEETH
This demonic creature is notable for its teeth which are made of iron and deliver a powerful bite.

FEET
The Asanbosam does not have normal feet but has hooks where its feet should be. It dangles these from trees to capture its prey.

LEGS
Many descriptions of this vampire say it has extremely long legs—long enough to sit in the treetops and still reach its victims on the forest floor.

The Asanbosam is a vampire creature from West African folktales. The Ashanti people of southern Ghana are very afraid of the Asanbosam. It takes a human form, apart from its grisly teeth and hooked legs, but feasts on the blood of people. It will hide in a tree and wait for a passerby to walk underneath, then hook and bite him on the thumb or big toe to drink his blood. After drinking its fill, the Asanbosam eats the victim's flesh. Sometimes, it plays with the victim for sport, in the way that a cat might play with a mouse.

Not all tree dwellers with hooked feet are Asanbosam. Watch out for the Naglopers—shape changers who can adapt their legs to mimic the hooks of the Asanbosam. Naglopers torture the victims they catch. Sometimes they transform their victims into the same shape, and force them to act out the Asanbosam legend. The Naglopers will only restore their victims to their proper shape if they do as they are told and capture innocent people with their hooked feet.

ACTUAL SIZE

DID YOU KNOW?

• The creature's name can be spelled in different ways: Asasabonsam and Asanbosam are two of them. However, it is a different kind of monster from the Sasabonsam, which has horns and wings.

• According to some tales, the Asanbosam looks human enough to pass as a person in poor light—although its feet are always a giveaway!

• These creatures are so feared that Ghanaian people are reluctant to talk about them. They are seen as an unholy creature, in league with the devil, and can bring bad luck to anyone who speaks their name.

• Many of these tales are told by hunters, as a warning to young boys who are learning to trap and catch their food. It is dangerous to travel in the forests alone, and the Asanbosam tale might teach them to be cautious.

WHERE IN THE WORLD?

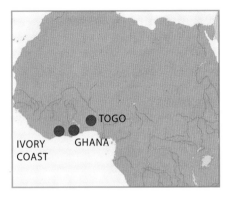

TOGO

IVORY COAST

GHANA

Asanbosam tales are most often told in southern Ghana, but the creature is also known in the neighboring countries of Togo and the Ivory Coast.

Baobhan Sith

FACE
The women commonly have green eyes and very pale skin and lips. They are unusually beautiful.

HAIR
Often blonde or ghostly white, their hair flows past their shoulders and helps to make them attractive.

CLOTHES
These evil creatures are most often seen wearing a long, green dress and a flowing cloak. Their garments often smell of blood.

NAILS
These vampiric ghosts don't have pointed teeth to suck blood: they pierce skin with very pointy fingernails and drink from the wounds.

FEET
The long robes hide their unusual feet, which take the form of the hooves of a deer.

Pronounced "baavan shee," baobhan sith are ghostly vampire-women and are thought to be related to the banshees of other Celtic myths. They usually gather in forests and wooded areas and often hang out in groups. Taking the form of beautiful women, they entice men to dance with them. Some say that they have hypnotic powers to help them do this. When the men are captivated by their dance, and too exhausted or entranced to fight back, the women pounce on them and feast on their blood. The victims are sucked dry and left for dead. A baobhan sith's feared substance is iron.

Four men were traveling through the forest, and stopped for the night in a clearing. They played music and danced, and one of the men wished that he had a female partner to dance with. Four beautiful women suddenly appeared. Three of them danced with the travelers, while the fourth stood with the musician. It was this man who noticed blood streaming from his friends. He ran and hid in their circle of horses. It was their iron horseshoes that protected him from the baobhan sith until morning.

ACTUAL SIZE

WHERE IN THE WORLD?

SCOTTISH HIGHLANDS

These delicate, dancing fiends are also known as the White Women of the Scottish Highlands.

DID YOU KNOW?

• The baobhan sith are often associated with another female demon, the succubus—a woman who seduces men in their sleep.

• Some stories say that the baobhan sith cannot bear sunlight, like many other types of vampire.

• It may be that tales of these evil beings were spread by human women to prevent their husbands from cheating on them.

• Baobhan sith usually prey on hunters who are away from home for a few days, or unsuspecting men who don't get home before darkness falls.

• The Japanese manga series *Hellsing* features baobhan sith, as do the fantasy books written by Mark Chadbourn.

Black Annis

EYE
In most versions of the tale, Black Annis has only a single eye in the middle of her face.

STRENGTH
Don't be fooled by her old lady appearance. Black Annis is extremely strong, and once she has you in her grip, there is no escape.

HANDS
The wizened crone has very long, strong fingers with claws instead of nails.

BODY
Black Annis is a shape shifter, and can change her form into that of a black cat. She is sometimes called "Cat Anna."

FACE
Black Annis is certainly noticeable, as she has wrinkled, blue skin and yellow fangs for teeth.

This evil crone was said to live in Leicestershire, England, in a cave that she carved out of the stone herself, using only her clawed fingers to gouge away the rock. Outside the cave was an old oak tree that provided an excellent hiding place for Black Annis. She waited for passersby, especially children, and then jumped out to catch them and drag them inside the cave. There, she skinned them alive and hung up the skins to dry. She feasted on the flesh and threw away the bones, but saved the dry skins to wear. If she became too hungry, she would resort to eating animals from local farms.

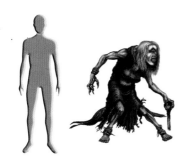

ACTUAL SIZE

Three children were sent out one day to collect firewood. They gathered as much as they could, but night began to fall, and they became afraid that Black Annis would get them. Sure enough, they heard shuffling and snuffling, and turned to see her behind them. They dropped their firewood and ran back home, but she caught up with them at their cottage door. Their father hit her with an ax and she turned to run, but was struck down by the sound of the holy church bells that had begun to ring out for Christmas.

WHERE IN THE WORLD?

LEICESTER

Black Annis is said to have lived in a cave, called Black Annis's Bower, just outside the city of Leicester in England.

DID YOU KNOW?

• **In Scotland, she is known as "Gentle Annie." It was thought that flattering her with a nice name would make her look kindly on people and leave them alone.**

• **For many years, the people of Leicester staged a mock hunt to celebrate the end of winter. They dragged a dead cat, soaked in aniseed, through the streets to signify Black Annis.**

• **The cave can no longer be seen. With the passing of time, it gradually filled up with earth, and was covered over just after World War I to build houses.**

• **Annis's growls and teeth-grinding were so loud that the townsfolk were warned if she was coming and could lock their doors and place herbs at the windows to prevent her from coming in.**

Boo Hag

EYES
It's unlikely you will ever look a boo hag in the eye—her victims are deep in slumber, after all. If you did wake, though, you would see hollow black pits where her eyes should be.

HAIR
The hag's flowing locks are long and as red as her body. Her hair stands on end, though, so it won't tickle and wake her sleeping victim.

SKIN
Strictly speaking, a boo hag has no skin of her own. She is bright red in appearance, because her muscles are on the outside. This makes her warm to the touch, like raw meat.

MOUTH
The gaping mouth in a boo hag's face is a horror-filled hole used to suck the breath from her victims.

Like vampires, boo hags roam in the night, looking for victims to feed on. However, the boo hag doesn't suck blood. She steals a person's breath by sucking it out of them while they sleep. This is known as "ridin'," and you might hear the warning "Don't let de hag ride ya" in areas where she hunts. The hag flies to her victim's house and enters through a crack or hole, such as a keyhole. As she sucks the breath, her prey sleeps soundly and dreamlessly. They won't know they've been ridden, although they will feel tired the next morning.

Boo hags are infamous for stealing human skin to disguise themselves. If a victim struggles and tries to wake, the boo hag will abandon the breath-sucking and strip the skin off their prey's body. Wearing it like baby's clothes, she can roam freely and choose her next victim. Before going ridin', she undresses from the skin and hides it for when she returns. There's one small catch, though. The boo hag must be back in the skin before dawn, or she will be trapped without skin forever.

ACTUAL SIZE

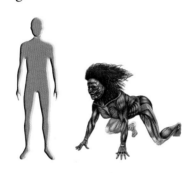

WHERE IN THE WORLD?

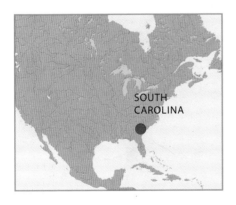

SOUTH CAROLINA

The boo hag goes "ridin'" in South Carolina.

DID YOU KNOW?

• To stay safe, it's said you should sleep with a broom by your bedside. The hags are distracted by counting the straws in the broom and run out of time to conduct their gruesome business.

• The African American communities of South Carolina tell the story of the boo hag, a Gullah legend. The Gullah language and culture still retain much from their African roots.

• In one tale, the boo hags marry unsuspecting men and deliver them to the "boo daddy," who eats their flesh. To get rid of the hag, her husband must fill her empty skin with salt and pepper, which will burn her raw, muscled body.

Bram Stoker's Dracula

AGE
Count Dracula is centuries old, but because of his bloodsucking habits he never ages. After he has feasted, he revitalizes. His white hair becomes darker, and his skin less pale.

HEAD
His ears are very pale and pointed at the top, his cheeks are pale and thin, and he has a mustache and bushy eyebrows that almost meet in the middle. His white hair is thinning at the front but thick everywhere else.

MOUTH
When the Count smiles, he reveals his pointed white teeth. He has a cruel mouth with unnaturally red lips.

HANDS
Jonathan Harker notices that the Count has hairs growing on the palms of his pale, broad hands. His nails are long and very pointed.

ount Dracula is the main character in Bram Stoker's 1897 book *Dracula*. He is a shape-shifting vampire who can change into various creatures such as a bat or a giant dog—and also into fog, to allow him to move into locked rooms. He holds Jonathan Harker prisoner in Castle Dracula, but keeps him alive for his own purposes. Harker nearly becomes the victim of three female vampires—the Count's wives—but the Count saves him. Dracula casts no reflection in a mirror, and cannot bear sunlight, garlic, or crosses. To kill him, he must be stabbed in the heart with a stake—then he crumbles to dust.

Although Dracula spares Harker's life, he is not so kind to Harker's fiancée, Mina, and her friend Lucy. Lucy becomes a vampire herself and has to be killed with a stake through the heart and then beheaded. Mina is bitten by Dracula, and he feeds her with his own blood to form a dangerous bond between them. Only when Dracula dies will Mina be free from this curse. A group of Lucy and Mina's friends track down Dracula, who has fled back to his home in Transylvania, and manage to kill him.

ACTUAL SIZE

WHERE IN THE WORLD?

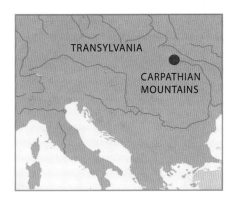

The Count lives in Castle Dracula in the Carpathian Mountains, on the border of Transylvania, Bukovina, and Moldavia.

DID YOU KNOW?

• When Harker stays at Castle Dracula, he is puzzled by the Count's behavior. He never eats or drinks, and he sleeps all day and works at night. Gradually, Harker begins to realize what sort of creature Dracula really is.

• At times, Harker sees Dracula climb out of a castle window and run down the stone walls just like a lizard, with his large cloak billowing around him.

• Parts of the novel are set in Whitby in Yorkshire, England, where Bram Stoker spent many vacations. In the story, Dracula sails to Whitby, devouring the ship's crew along the way.

• Dracula dies in his coffin but not with a stake through the heart. He has his throat cut and his heart stabbed with a knife—but is that enough to finish him off forever, or could the Count rise again one day?

Chupacabra

SKIN
Usually described as gray in color, the chupacabra may have scaly, reptilian skin or mangy, patchy fur. It has spines down its back.

EYES
The eyes are large and mean. They are usually reported as being black or bright red.

MOUTH
The chupacabra's mouth looks like a small slit that fails to cover the fangs sticking out from its upper and lower jaws.

HANDS
Both hands have three fingers and a thumb with strong claws at the end of each one.

COLOR
It's said that the chupacabra can change color like a chameleon. It may look green when seen in sunny clearings or dark brown in the middle of a forest.

MOVEMENT
Reports vary about how the chupacabra gets around. Most agree that it moves on two feet. Some say it jumps like a kangaroo—up to 20 feet (6 m) in a single leap. Others even claim it can fly.

The name chupacabra means "goat sucker," and this vampiric creature has a particular liking for goats. Its victims include livestock and pets. Its prey is usually found completely drained of blood. Two or three puncture marks are the telltale sign of the chupacabra. Whether these are made with its two largest fangs or its three claws, no one is sure. The holes are perfectly round and sometimes large enough to insert a human finger. Sometimes, the unfortunate animal has its internal organs mutilated or eaten, with no obvious wounds where the organs could have been removed.

Organized groups of chupacabra hunters sometimes gather to track down the creature and prevent the mutilation of their livestock. It is believed that the chupacabras live in caves, and some farmers find the cave entrances and start fires to burn the creatures out. Farmers have shot the creature attacking their animals, but these have turned out to be wild dogs and coyotes. Chupacabras' pronounced backbones and unusually long teeth and claws make them look more like an alien creature than the canines they are.

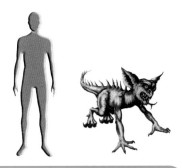

ACTUAL
SIZE

WHERE IN THE WORLD?

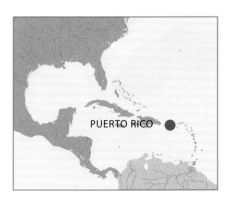

PUERTO RICO

Originally reported in Puerto Rico, there have been chupacabra attacks from the United States down to Brazil and Chile.

DID YOU KNOW?

• According to legend, the chupacabra has a forked tongue and leaves behind a strong smell of sulfur, making people feel sick.

• One theory suggests that the chupacabras are aliens because of their large oval heads and huge eyes. Some say the creatures are the result of a scientific crossbreeding between animals and aliens.

• The chupacabra is the main creature in the Scooby Doo movie *The Monster of Mexico*.

• Puerto Rico already had its own vampire: El Vampiro de Moco, which worked in a similar way to the chupacabra. This vampire also drained its victims of blood. Eventually it was suggested that these vampires were actually crocodiles that had been illegally released.

Edward Cullen

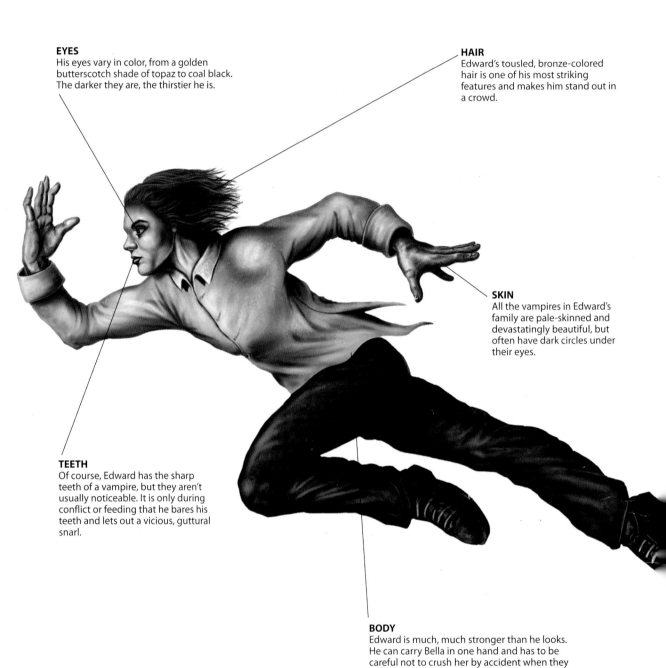

EYES
His eyes vary in color, from a golden butterscotch shade of topaz to coal black. The darker they are, the thirstier he is.

HAIR
Edward's tousled, bronze-colored hair is one of his most striking features and makes him stand out in a crowd.

SKIN
All the vampires in Edward's family are pale-skinned and devastatingly beautiful, but often have dark circles under their eyes.

TEETH
Of course, Edward has the sharp teeth of a vampire, but they aren't usually noticeable. It is only during conflict or feeding that he bares his teeth and lets out a vicious, guttural snarl.

BODY
Edward is much, much stronger than he looks. He can carry Bella in one hand and has to be careful not to crush her by accident when they embrace.

The Cullen family is an unusual breed of modern vampire. They choose not to drink human blood and prey only upon wild animals. Edward's favorite is the mountain lion, but his brother Emmett prefers grizzly bear. They live a relatively normal life, attending high school or working in the community, but are aloof and otherworldly. They are all very strong and can move at lightning speed. Both of these skills help in their hunt for a meal. Add to that their venomous bite and their physical attractiveness, and it's easy to see how they have survived for centuries.

ACTUAL SIZE

Edward meets Bella when she moves to live with her father. He is drawn to her, even though he knows it could be fatal for her. He is attracted by her smell. Something about her scent appeals to his taste buds. He tries to overcome his feelings as a vampire to allow them to develop their relationship. When they finally allow themselves to be alone together, Edward has to overcome the strong urges he feels as he touches Bella's neck and strokes her skin. But is the real danger from Edward, or from the vampires in his company?

WHERE IN THE WORLD?

WASHINGTON

Edward and his family live in the small town of Forks, Washington, where it is often cloudy.

DID YOU KNOW?

• Edward's adoptive father, Carlisle, is a doctor. He works with blood and human bodies every day, but is so settled in his animal-only ways that he is never tempted by the human blood.

• These vampires aren't afraid of the sun, but glitter like diamonds in the sunlight, so they stay in the shade to avoid attracting attention.

• All of the vampires have superheightened senses, but Edward has the additional ability to hear people's thoughts if they are close enough to him.

• There are very few ways to kill these vampires. The best way is to tear him or her to shreds and then burn the pieces.

Eli

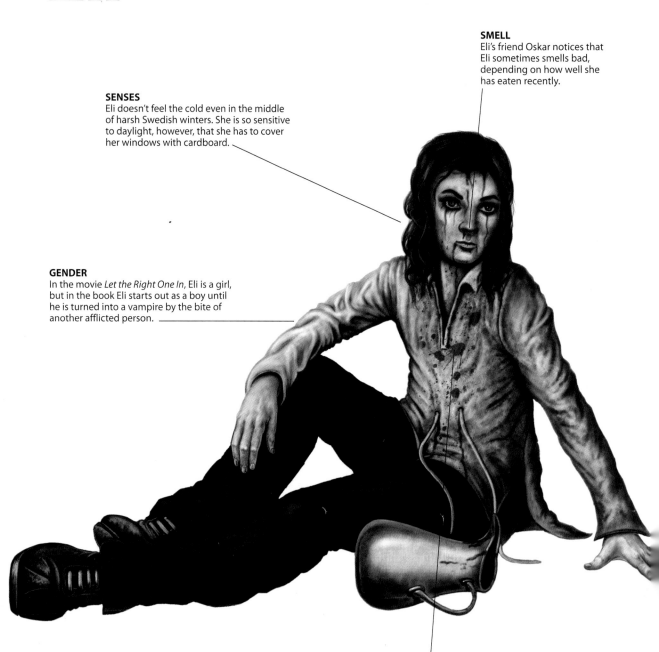

SMELL
Eli's friend Oskar notices that Eli sometimes smells bad, depending on how well she has eaten recently.

SENSES
Eli doesn't feel the cold even in the middle of harsh Swedish winters. She is so sensitive to daylight, however, that she has to cover her windows with cardboard.

GENDER
In the movie *Let the Right One In*, Eli is a girl, but in the book Eli starts out as a boy until he is turned into a vampire by the bite of another afflicted person.

BLOOD
As a vampire, Eli cannot walk uninvited into a person's home. When Oskar puts this to the test, Eli begins to bleed in patches all over her body.

Eli is a vampire, trying to live an ordinary life in an apartment block in Sweden. Ordinary, that is, except for her guardian Håkan, who has to hunt down victims and drain their blood for Eli to drink. Eli becomes friends with her neighbor, a boy named Oskar. He sees her true nature when she laps up his blood after he cuts his palm in an offer to become "blood brothers." They remain friends, though, and Eli helps Oskar fight back against bullies. At first, she helps in a human way, but by the end she goes on a killing frenzy, slaughtering three of the people who have been picking on Oskar.

Håkan sometimes struggles to get enough blood to feed Eli. When he can, he gives the victims anesthetic to paralyze them, then hangs them upside down and cuts their throat. He collects the blood in a jug for Eli to drink. However, his first attempts to prey on people in their new home are failures, and Eli starts to feel hungry and weak. Håkan eventually offers her his own blood, straight from his neck. After Eli has drunk her fill, Håkan falls from a tall building and dies, leaving Eli to fend for herself.

ACTUAL SIZE

WHERE IN THE WORLD?

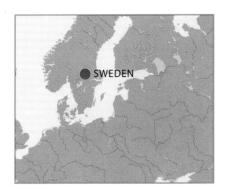

SWEDEN

Eli and Håkan move into the apartment next door to Oskar in the Swedish town of Stockholm.

DID YOU KNOW?

• Eli's victim Virginia is turned into a vampire herself after she is bitten by Eli. Rather than endure this fiendish life, she kills herself. As vampires cannot bear sunlight, she opens the blinds of her room in broad daylight and bursts into flames.

• Among Eli's supernatural, vampiric powers is the ability to climb the outside of buildings and to flit from window to window, even two stories up.

• Oskar is 12 years old and thinks that Eli is around the same age, but when he asks she can't remember her birth date. It is only when Oskar realizes what she really is that he figures out why Eli doesn't celebrate a birthday.

• Eli and Oskar appear in the novel *Let the Right One In* by Swedish author John Ajvide Lindqvist. Lindqvist also wrote the screenplay for the movie.

Elizabeth Bathory

SKIN
Her skin was pale, clear, and blemish-free, and she was very proud of its youthful appearance.

MIND
Elizabeth's beautiful exterior kept her wicked interior hidden from the world. Few could imagine that a gorgeous woman was capable of such evil acts.

FACE
The Countess was often spoken about because of her beauty, and it was the desire to keep this reputation that made her look for unusual and gruesome beauty products.

TEETH
Not as you would expect—these are not the teeth of a vampire. But the tales of her bloodlust suggest that Bram Stoker knew her story when he was writing *Dracula*.

CLOTHES
The noble classes from this period of history wore colorful, fine outfits with many layers and ruffles. Their jewels showed others how rich they were.

Elizabeth Bathory wasn't the invention of a writer, but a real noblewoman who was born in the sixteenth century. She lived in a castle with her faithful servants who assisted her with her evil crimes: capturing and torturing young girls. It is said that Elizabeth held as many as 600 young women captive, and she is often known as "The Blood Countess." She took great delight in causing pain and humiliating her victims, but her crimes escalated when she began to believe that their blood would help to preserve her youth and beauty. This idea was confirmed by her servants, who were rumored to be witches.

ACTUAL
SIZE

Legend says that Elizabeth sat in her bedroom having her hair styled, and her nervous servant pulled her hair and hurt Elizabeth's head. Elizabeth flew into a rage, and smacked the girl so hard that blood flew, landing upon Elizabeth's hand. She thought that it had an instant effect on her skin, making it look younger. But that wasn't enough for the wicked Countess. She began to kill her victims so that she could take a bath in their blood. She may even have drunk their blood like a vampire to feel its full effect.

WHERE IN THE WORLD?

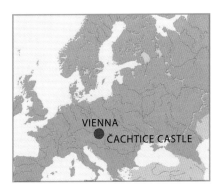

VIENNA
ČACHTICE CASTLE

The Countess committed most of her crimes at Čachtice Castle, but moved to Vienna in Austria when she thought she had been found out.

DID YOU KNOW?

• Born in Hungary, Elizabeth's true name was Báthory Erzsébet. Elizabeth is the English form of the name.

• As a child, Elizabeth may have been mentally ill, leading to her fiendish behavior as an adult. She was used to witnessing cruel acts of punishment: one story describes a thief who was caught and sewn into the belly of a dying horse, with only his head out, and left like that until he died.

• At first, the Countess chose servants and peasants as her victims and carried out her crimes for years without being accused. Her evil deeds could no longer be ignored when she began to attack young noble girls.

• Elizabeth was eventually held prisoner in her own castle. She was walled into her bedchamber, with only slits left for air and food, and died there after about three years.

Impundulu

FEATHERS
The bird's feathers are pure white, in contrast to its legs and beak. Other accounts describe it as having a body covered in a rainbow of colored feathers.

BEAK
The impundulu's beak is vivid scarlet—the color of blood.

LEGS
The huge talons enable the impundulu to hold down victims while feeding on them.

WINGS
Watch out for the wings! They can shoot out bolts of electricity, like lightning, from their feathered ends.

This bird is the size of a man, with mighty wings that produce lightning from the tips. It can create thunder with a flap of these wings, and it's said that forked lightning is the bird's droppings falling from the sky. The impundulu feeds on human blood, holding onto its victims with its fearsome talons. It has an almost unquenchable thirst. The birds are kept as servants, or familiars, by witches and witch doctors, and sent out to attack their enemies. The creatures are also used to spread disease and infection. A faithful familiar will be handed down through a family of witches.

Young women are the favorite victim of the impundulu. In order to capture them, the bird takes on the form of an attractive young man, who charms the young women until they are easy prey. If he is successful, the woman may become his slave or even be turned into a witch. The men are recognizable through their disguise by "witch sniffers," who are able to detect a witch or a witch's familiar in whatever form.

ACTUAL SIZE

WHERE IN THE WORLD?

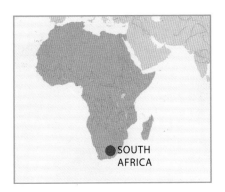

SOUTH AFRICA

Tales of the impundulu are told across South Africa by tribes such as the Zulu, Pondo, and Xhosa.

DID YOU KNOW?

• This bird is almost impossible to destroy. If you catch it, it should be burned to death to prevent it from coming back to life.

• Some local healers possess a special magical cream or lotion made from impundulu fat, which protects its wearers from an attack by the creature.

• The impundulu is linked to illnesses that involve excessisve bleeding.

• The bird's name translates as "lightning bird." It uses owls and eagles, which are seen as evil omens of death, as its servants.

• Said to be the most evil of a witch's familiars, the impundulu has strong magic. If it sees blood, it becomes frenzied and will attack any humans nearby.

Jiang Shi

FINGERNAILS
The fingernails are black, long, and razor sharp. This could be the result of being dead for a long time, or from being buried underground.

ARMS
Like all dead bodies, jiang shi suffer from rigor mortis (the stiffening of a body after death). This makes them walk with their arms stretched out in front of them.

LEGS
Their legs become stiff after death, which makes walking difficult. Instead, jiang shi move with a stiff, strange jumping motion.

CLOTHING
It can take a long time for a body to become a jiang shi, so their clothes are usually very old-fashioned.

The name "jiang shi" is Chinese for "stiff corpse." Like zombies, jiang shi are dead bodies that can move and hunt down humans. These creatures search for blood and have an endless hunger for it. They also murder people and feed on their life essence as it seeps out. Jiang shi are brain-dead and cannot think, see, or speak, but they seek out their prey either with their sense of smell or by detecting their breathing. It is said that holding your breath might be the difference between capture and escape if you are confronted by one of these monsters.

Tales of jiang shi originate from the Chinese custom of transporting dead people back to their hometown to be buried. Priests were paid to carry them and often brought back several corpses at a time, lined up on bamboo rods, which made them look like they were hopping along by themselves. A true jiang shi is only created if the person was particularly wicked while alive.

ACTUAL SIZE

WHERE IN THE WORLD?

CHINA

Jiang shi are said to travel alone or in groups across China, sometimes covering hundreds of miles to return to their hometown.

DID YOU KNOW?

• To ward off a jiang shi, you need to write a special spell on thin yellow paper, using chicken's blood as ink, and stick it to its forehead.

• It is also said that rice will stop jiang shi in their tracks. They cannot pass by without stopping to count every single grain. Sticky rice can be used to draw out their evil spirit.

• Jiang shi can be gathered together by an evil master and used as an army of the walking dead. They are sometimes put to work as bodyguards or can be sent into battle against an enemy.

• Sometimes, jiang shi keep decaying, continuing to look more and more decomposed and terrifying.

BLOODSUCKING BEASTS

Jikininki

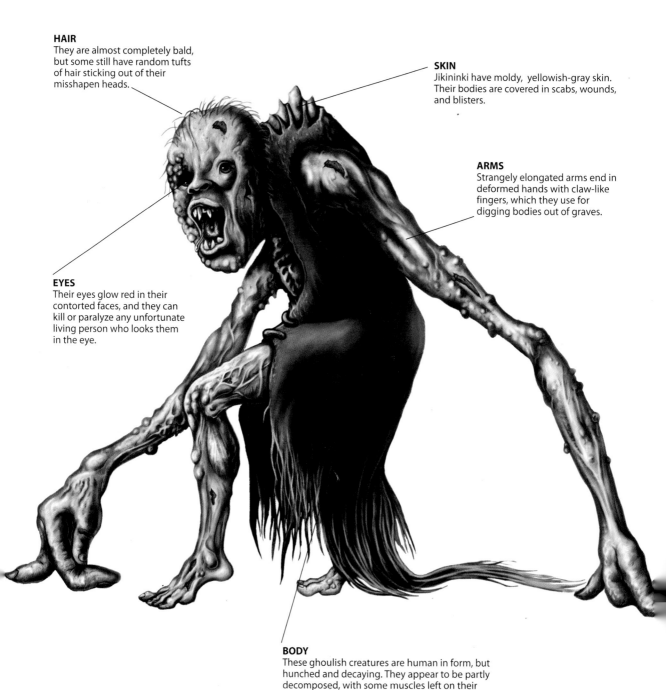

HAIR
They are almost completely bald, but some still have random tufts of hair sticking out of their misshapen heads.

SKIN
Jikininki have moldy, yellowish-gray skin. Their bodies are covered in scabs, wounds, and blisters.

ARMS
Strangely elongated arms end in deformed hands with claw-like fingers, which they use for digging bodies out of graves.

EYES
Their eyes glow red in their contorted faces, and they can kill or paralyze any unfortunate living person who looks them in the eye.

BODY
These ghoulish creatures are human in form, but hunched and decaying. They appear to be partly decomposed, with some muscles left on their thinning bodies.

Jikininki are Japanese ghosts or undead who feast on human corpses. They move around at night, raiding graveyards. In some tales, they can disguise themselves as normal human beings during the day. They are the spirits of people who lived greedy or selfish lives and are cursed to remain undead as punishment for their sins. Most of them realize the horrors of what they do, and hate the constant hunger they have for human flesh. They cannot speak, but can grunt and squeal like wild animals. Many have jagged teeth for tearing at flesh and bones.

ACTUAL
SIZE

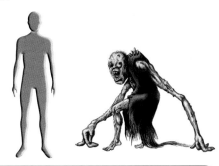

A priest called Muso was witness to the horrible actions of a Jikininki. Being lost, he sought help from a village, where the people kindly gave him food and shelter. However, they said that a man had died that day and it was tradition that they must stay away from the village all night. Muso stayed behind, and was performing his priestly duties by the dead body when an evil spirit entered the room. Muso could not speak or move, but watched in horror as the dark shape lifted up the body and ate it, bones and all.

WHERE IN THE WORLD?

Jikininki are nomadic scavengers, constantly roaming the countryside to raid new graves. They are found mostly in Japan, but also in other parts of Asia.

DID YOU KNOW?

• Jikininki may steal from the bodies they eat, wearing their clothes and using any valuables they find to bribe important people to leave them alone.

• These greedy monsters hide behind tombstones or within shallow graves. They don't like to be seen, but if disturbed they will fight. Their claws and teeth are dangerous weapons, and any living person who is wounded by one may become infected with the Jikininki curse.

• The undead are hard to destroy. They cannot be poisoned or injured and they do not bleed.

• Jikininki are a form of "rakshasa," a Buddhist or Hindu demon. They can be put to rest with religious ceremonies called "segaki," which means "feeding the hungry ghosts."

Mandurugo

FACE
During the daytime, the mandurugo is a beautiful woman. Her features become twisted and evil when she flies out at night looking for food.

WINGS
To get around, the mandurugo has a pair of wings attached to its body.

EYES
The eyes are bloodshot as a result of staying up all night in search of prey.

TONGUE
It uses a long, hollow tongue to suck the blood from its victims.

BODY
A mandurugo can detach the top half of its body from its bottom half, which it leaves standing and must return to by morning.

There are many tales of vampires told in the Philippines, but most have common features. The mandurugo is a beautiful female with a taste for blood. She can detach the upper half of her body from her legs, and grow wings at night to fly off in search of her next victim. She makes a strange "wak-wak" or "tik-tik" noise that is louder the farther away she is. As the sound becomes quieter, it confuses her victims into thinking she is moving away, when actually she is getting closer. She lands on the thatched roof of a house while the people are sleeping. She pokes the victim's skin with her tongue to drink his or her blood.

ACTUAL SIZE

On an island lived a very beautiful woman. She married, but within a year her husband withered away and died. She took another husband, and he died in the same manner. Her third husband also died after just one year. She took a fourth husband, but he was wise to her true nature. He pretended to be asleep, but when he felt something pricking his neck, he took a knife and stabbed the thing on top of him. He heard it fly away into the night. The next day his wife was found dead from a stab wound.

WHERE IN THE WORLD?

PHILIPPINES

The Philippines are made up of many islands, and most of them have their own variation of the mandurugo horror story.

DID YOU KNOW?

• These creatures are also called "wak-waks" or "tik-tiks" (because of the noise they make). They can also be called "aswangs" or "manananggals," depending on which island the tales are told.

• The word "mandurugo" means "bloodsucker." "Manananggal" translates as "separated one."

• Variations in the folklore say that these creatures may have a black chick in their throat, which gives them their evil power, or that they are accompanied by wicked night birds that lead them to the home of their next victim.

• If you can prevent the creature from returning to its bottom half, it will die. You can sprinkle salt on the severed legs, or swap the legs to confuse the top halves.

Mara

WINGS
Not everyone agrees whether mara has wings or not—after all, her victims are always sleeping.

BODY
Although weighty enough to trap her victims, in appearance the mara seems light, floaty, and almost see-through.

MOUTH
A nightmarish vision, the mara has an ordinary mouth filled with vicious fangs.

FINGERS
She has long, slender fingers that she entwines in the manes of horses and even the branches of trees.

In Scandinavia, the local version of the night hag is called the mara. She is a spirit being who seems shadowy until she sits on the chests of her sleeping victims, when she can weigh them down so they are unable to move. The mara can seep into a bedroom through a keyhole or a crack underneath the door. Like the boo hag, she is said to "ride" her victims, but she feeds on their blood while she is riding. It is said that the spirit of any sleeping woman can slip out into the night and become a mara, if the woman is cursed or simply wicked enough.

A mara does not necessarily need human blood to feed upon. She is also partial to the blood of horses. She grabs onto their manes, leaving them tangled and knotted the next morning as evidence that she has been there. These twisted knots are known as "marelocks." The poor horses are left exhausted, frightened, and bathed in sweat when their owners find them. It is also said that a tree with extremely tangled branches is a sign that a mara is roaming the area.

ACTUAL SIZE

WHERE IN THE WORLD?

SCANDINAVIA

The mara works her wickedness in Scandinavia, but she is also known to be seen and felt by sleeping people in other parts of western Europe.

DID YOU KNOW?

• The word "nightmare" comes from "mara," as the sleeping person usually feels her presence in the form of tormented dreams that are difficult to wake up from.

• Other countries also get their word for nightmare from this hag: *nachtmerrie* (Netherlands), *mareridt* (Denmark), *cauchemar* (France), *mardraum*, or *mareritt* (Norway), *martrö* (Iceland), and *mardröm* (Sweden).

• A woman suspected of being a mara can often be cured by confronting her and saying "You are a mara" three times over before she runs away.

• In Denmark, the name "mara" is used for all female vampires. In some other countries, the mara has no fangs, but frightens her victims and feeds off their fear.

Nocnitsa

FACE
Hidden in shadow, it is hard to see her face, except for her fangs and the two dots of light that make up her eyes.

HEIGHT
Nocnitsa isn't tall, and looks even shorter because she is hunched over, applying all of her weight to her victim's chest.

LIGHT
Appearing only at night, Nocnitsa seems to consist of flickering shadows, and her lower body trails away into wisps of darkness.

HANDS
Old and gnarled, her hands are crippled with age, and she has vicious talons instead of nails.

Like other nightmarish visions from different parts of the globe, the Nocnitsa creeps into the bedrooms of dreaming people. She sits on their chests, and their dreams are filled with the feeling of being pinned down so they cannot move from their own bed. She is also known as the night hag. She preys on children, so it is quite easy for her to keep them still with her body weight, even though she is small. Nocnitsa has a distinct smell of wet moss, soil, and fir trees. This may invade her victim's dreams or linger in the bedroom the morning after her visit.

ACTUAL SIZE

Nocnitsa is particularly frightening for parents with young children. They believe that their precious ones might wake screaming from their nightmares—or worse, never wake up at all. To protect them, they draw a circle around the child's crib with the point of a knife. Some even leave the knife under the mattress, as it is thought that the metal protects the child. It is also claimed that placing a protective doll or an ax under the floorboards beneath the crib can keep Nocnitsa away.

WHERE IN THE WORLD?

RUSSIA

POLAND

BULGARIA

Nocnitsa tales are common in eastern Europe, including Poland, Russia, and Bulgaria.

DID YOU KNOW?

• **If you find a stone with a hole in it, keep it as protection from Nocnitsa. It can be hung by your bed at night and worn around your neck in the daytime.**

• **In Bulgaria, Nocnitsa is known as Gorska Makua. In Poland, she is Krisky or Plaksy. Whatever her name, no good ever comes from her visits, and children are warned to go to sleep quickly and quietly, without fuss and tantrums, so they stay safe and have sweet dreams.**

• **No one has ever heard her speak, but she can screech and yowl if she is threatened.**

• **It is not known where Nocnitsa goes in the daytime. She may hide in the forests, or have a concealed home—or she may simply disappear when the sun rises.**

Penanggalan

ODOR
Even in human form, the penanggalan smells of vinegar, as she uses so much of it to preserve her decapitated body and to soak her entrails.

HAIR
She grows her hair long, adding to the effect of looking like an octopus when she moves.

FANGS
The penanggalan all have vicious fangs. Many tales say they also have a very long, invisible tongue, which they use to suck blood.

34

The penanggalan is a Malaysian vampire who is instantly recognizable. By day, she looks like a normal woman—usually a beautiful one, having used witchcraft to enhance her looks. By night, she leaves her body behind, and flies around houses as only a head. She is in search of human blood to drink, and sometimes flesh to eat. She prefers the blood of young children and hangs around screeching while a child is born. She sucks blood with her long, invisible tongue poking into the house. Her victims are not killed instantly but die slowly from disease.

ACTUAL
SIZE

One day, a woman was bathing in a large wooden vat of vinegar. This may have been as a penance, or she may have been meditating, but whatever the reason, she was so caught up in her thoughts that she did not hear a man approach. When he asked the woman what she was doing, she was startled out of her trance. She moved her head up to look at him so quickly that it was ripped off from her body, and the head flew away to a nearby tree.

WHERE IN THE WORLD?

MALAY PENINSULA

The penanggalan does her wicked work around the Malay Peninsula, a hot area where the houses are commonly built on stilts, allowing her access through the floorboards.

DID YOU KNOW?

• A penanggalan's entrails are said to glow at night, like fireflies.

• Many stories say that the creatures are midwives who are in league with the devil.

• To stop a penanggalan from entering your house, you must plant a special thorny plant to grow around the windows and doors. You can also grow spiky pineapples in the space between the ground and the house, which is on stilts, to stop her from coming up through the floorboards.

• While flying at night, the creature's body is left in a vat of vinegar to preserve it. One of the best ways to destroy it is to place glass in the neck, to slash the entrails as they return to their body. They are also vulnerable to ash or crushed garlic if placed in the body.

Rokurokubi

NECK
A Rokurokubi's defining feature is its extremely long neck that can be stretched away from the body and act independently.

HEAD
Even if separated from its body, the head can be identified as that of a Rokurokubi by a series of red characters at the base of the neck stump.

FACE
By day, the Rokurokubi's face is that of a normal person, but when it leaves its body behind it can transform into the frightening face of an ogre.

SPEECH
They can still speak normally when their head is stretched far from their body. Some Rokurokubi hang out together at night.

These creatures are one of the strangest-looking beings in Japanese folklore. By day, they live as normal humans, but at night they can stretch their necks like a garden hose to allow their heads to roam freely. Sometimes they are simply mischief makers, frightening people who are out late at night. The more sinister ones among them prey on people, sucking their blood and even eating them. A few Rokurokubi don't know what they turn into at night. Their only clue is strange dreams where they feel they are looking down on the world from a great height or a curious angle.

There is a tale of an ex-Samurai who becomes a priest and travels around his country. One night, he is invited to sleep in a hut. He gets up for a drink and is shocked to see five Rokurokubi bodies in the main room, each of them headless. Nevertheless, he is a brave man and takes action. He knows that the creatures can be killed by removing the body so its head cannot return. He watches one lost head as it bounces on the floor three times and then dies.

ACTUAL
SIZE

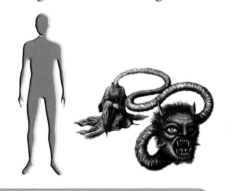

WHERE IN THE WORLD?

JAPAN

Watch out for Rokurokubi in all parts of Japan. They live in towns and cities as well as in quiet rural villages.

DID YOU KNOW?

• **Rokurokubi are a form of Japanese yokai, which means "bewitching apparition." They usually appear at dawn and dusk.**

• **Some of these creatures reveal themselves only to wicked or irreligious people. Others play it safe and let themselves be seen only by humans who will not be believed when they tell their tales, such as drunkards or fools.**

• **It is said that these monsters are created from people who do not follow the teachings of the Buddhist religion properly.**

• **It is possible for a Rokurokubi to live a normal life during the day and to get married and have children. Their husbands or wives only rarely find out, if they wake to find their partner's head high on a window ledge or door frame.**

Strigoi

FACE
A strigoi will show signs of being undead around the face: it may simply be pale and washed out, or more frightening with hollow, red-rimmed eyes and traces of blood from its feeding frenzies.

HEARTS
Strigoi are often said to have two hearts next to each other.

CLOTHES
If a strigoi has risen from the grave, this is often apparent by the decayed state of its clothing.

HANDS
Bony, skeletal hands and dirty, broken fingernails are telltale signs that the strigoi has been buried underground.

ANIMAL FORM
Some strigoi steal the form of an animal—usually a cat, dog, or sheep—and can transform themselves into this shape to leave their own body at night.

The strigoi is an evil force that is difficult to get rid of. The strigoi are usually troubled souls that rise from the grave to seek justice for something wrong done to them during their lifetime. They are thirsty for blood and can spend many nights hunting for food. They have to return to their grave regularly until they become older and stronger, when they only have to return to it every Saturday. If a strigoi is not destroyed after seven years, it no longer has to return to its grave and can move to live wherever it likes, looking like any normal person.

ACTUAL SIZE

WHERE IN THE WORLD?

TRANSYLVANIA

ROMANIA

The strigoi are famous in Romanian mythology. The area of Transylvania, famous in many vampire stories, is in Romania.

After rising from their grave, the strigoi pass through different stages. In its first stage, it is like a poltergeist, moving furniture and causing trouble in its old home. At this stage, it is invisible and often steals human food to eat. After this, it returns to the form it had when alive: visible, although sometimes the worse for wear after being buried. It feeds on livestock until it is strong enough to become a true undead creature. Even then, it still torments its family, choosing family members as its first victims and feeding on their blood.

DID YOU KNOW?

• Sometimes strigoi are known as "moroi," most often in the countryside.

• Strigoi can be tricked into leaving their victims alone by scattering seeds with a nail hidden within. The obsessive creatures cannot pass without counting the seeds. The hidden nail will prick them and force them to start counting all over again.

• Some types of strigoi can leave their body in the form of a spark of light that can zoom through the air.

• Most strigoi drink blood directly from their victim's heart. Their own hearts (although they have two) are their vulnerable spot: they can be killed by driving a stake through them.

• It used to be thought that an unmarried person would return from death as a strigoi and prey upon their former lovers.

Vlad Dracul

FACE
His face betrayed little of his nature: he was stern and wore a mustache, but might only strike fear into the hearts of those who had heard of his reputation.

AGE
Vlad was born in 1431 and died in 1476, when he was 45 years old.

HAIR
Vlad had extremely long, dark hair that billowed behind him when he rode his horse into battle.

CLOTHING
Vlad was a prince and therefore wore fine clothes, in keeping with the Romanian fashions of the 1400s.

VLAD DRACUL

A real prince from the fifteenth century, Vlad III was the son of "Vlad the Dragon," called "Vlad Dracul" in his own language. Vlad III thus gained the surname "Draculea," or "Son of Dragon." He is most famous as being the inspiration for Bram Stoker's title character in the 1897 novel *Dracula*. However, Vlad was not a vampire, merely a determined and fierce warrior. His favorite method of torturing and killing his enemies was impaling them on a stake, earning him the nickname Vlad the Impaler. He was Prince of Wallachia, an area in the south of Romania, but lived in Transylvania, with its rich history of vampires.

ACTUAL SIZE

Vlad was certainly a heartless man where his enemies were concerned. He killed many thousands of people during his attempts to defend his country against invasion by the Ottoman Empire. One army, on the march toward Wallachia, was stopped in its tracks by a mass of stakes with bodies impaled on them. It is thought that 20,000 Turkish prisoners were put on display to warn any other would-be attackers. Vlad is also said to have burned and boiled people, and had their hats nailed to their heads.

WHERE IN THE WORLD?

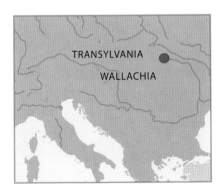

Vlad the Impaler lived in Transylvania, was the ruler of Wallachia, and fought against Hungarians and Turks from the Ottoman Empire.

DID YOU KNOW?

• Although he was known for his exceedingly cruel punishments, Vlad is mostly seen by the Romanians as a national savior. His methods were questionable, but he was loyal and successfully defended their country.

• It is thought that Bram Stoker read Vlad's name when he was researching Transylvania for vampire folklore. The cruel, bloody character fits the bill (although Vlad's love of stakes wasn't shared by vampires!).

• Vlad's Romanian name is Vlad (short for Vladislav) Tepes.

• Vlad was killed in battle. His head was chopped off and sent to the Turkish sultan as proof that Vlad the Impaler was actually dead. The Sultan had it put on a stake, a rather fitting end for a man of Vlad's habits.

Vrykolakas

LIGHT SENSITIVITY
Unlike many vampires, vrykolakes can roam in daylight hours without harmful effects, although they are most active at night.

FACE
Despite having been buried underground for several years, the face still has a reddish complexion.

BODY
You would expect a body to decay once it is buried, but the vrykolakes do not show signs of deterioration.

WEIGHT
The bodies look bloated and even fatter than when they were alive, which is said to be a result of drinking their fill of blood.

A vrykolakas (plural vrykolakes) is a dead person who has become a vampire. Throughout much of Greek history, burial sites were hard to find because the islands are so small. Three years after death, bodies had to be dug up so the bones could be removed and the ground used again. If a grave was opened and the body had not decayed, it was believed to be a vrykolakas. It was said this happened for religious reasons (being excommunicated, living an unholy life, or being buried in unconsecrated ground), but eating meat from a sheep that has been wounded by a werewolf may also turn you into a vrykolakas.

ACTUAL SIZE

WHERE IN THE WORLD?

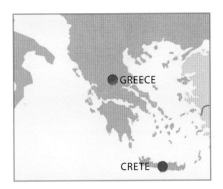

GREECE

CRETE

The vrykolakes are well known throughout Greece. On the island of Crete they are more often called Kathakano.

A village on the island of Crete lived in fear of a vrykolakas. They knew which graveyard it came from but not which grave. One night, a shepherd took shelter in the graveyard. As he placed his guns by his side to rest, they formed a cross. When the vampire tried to get past that night, the cross stopped him. He and the shepherd argued, and the next day the brave shepherd showed the villagers which grave held the evil creature. It was dug up and a priest was brought to make the undead body holy again.

DID YOU KNOW?

• A person can become a vrykolakas if a cat jumps over his dead body before it is buried.

• The name "vrykolakas" is sometimes used specifically for shepherds who have turned into vampires and feed on people and sheep when the moon is full.

• It is said that vrykolakes cannot cross seawater, so any that are captured are reburied on a deserted island to keep the human race safe.

• The creatures can be found and destroyed by a Sabbatarian (someone born on a Saturday, which gives them special holy powers) and their Fetch dog. If you see a dog on its own, be kind to it, as Sabbatarians can become invisible and may be watching over their precious dog without you knowing.

GUIDE TO BLOODSUCKING BEASTS

Asanbosam
Area: Southern Ghana, Togo, Ivory Coast
Features: Very long legs; hooks for feet; iron teeth; tail that ends in the head of a snake

Baobhan Sith
Area: Scottish Highlands
Features: Very beautiful face with pale skin and lips; green eyes; blonde or white hair; hooves for feet; very pointy fingernails; flowing dress and robes

Black Annis
Area: In a cave called Black Annis's Bower in Leicester, England
Features: Wrinkled blue skin; yellow fangs; single eye in center of forehead; claws instead of nails; can change into a black cat

Boo Hag
Area: South Carolina
Features: Hollow black pits for eyes; flowing red hair; muscled body with no skin; gaping hole for a mouth

Bram Stoker's Dracula
Area: Castle Dracula in the Carpathian Mountains, on the border of Transylvania
Features: Very pale skin; pointed ears; mustache and bushy eyebrows; pointy white teeth; white hair that becomes darker after feasting on blood

Chupacabra
Area: Puerto Rico, United States, Brazil, Chile
Features: Gray, reptilian skin that can change color (sometimes with patchy fur); spines along back; large eyes that are black or bright red; fanged jaws; strong claws

Edward Cullen
Area: Forks, Washington State
Features: Pale skin that sparkles in sunlight; topaz-colored eyes that turn black when thirsty for blood; tousled bronze hair; unusually strong body; fangs that are not usually visible

Eli
Area: Stockholm, Sweden
Features: Sensitive to daylight; smells bad when she hasn't eaten; bleeds from patches all over her body when she walks into a home she was not invited into

Elizabeth Bathory
Area: Čachtice Castle in Hungary; Vienna, Austria
Features: Very beautiful; pale, unblemished skin; layered, colorful gowns and many jewels

Impundulu
Area: South Africa
Features: Large bird with pure white or rainbow-colored feathers; blood-red beak; huge talons; wings that can shoot electricity; can take the form of a handsome young man to attract women

Jiang Shi

Area: China

Features: A dead body suffering from rigor mortis; arms are stretched out in front of it; long, black, razor-sharp fingernails; old-fashioned clothing; stiff legs that move with a jumping walk

Jikininki

Area: Japan, Philippines, Borneo

Features: Decaying human body; very long arms with claw-like fingers; moldy, yellow-gray skin; almost bald; eyes glow red

Mandurugo

Area: Philippines

Features: Detaches the top half of the body from the bottom half; wings; bloodshot eyes; has a beautiful woman's face during the day, which twists into evil and ugly at night; long, hollow tongue used to suck a victim's blood

Mara

Area: Scandinavia

Features: A light, almost see-through appearance; sometimes has wings; a mouth filled with fangs; long, slender fingers

Nocnitsa

Area: eastern Europe

Features: Small, shadowy body; two dots of light for eyes; gnarled hands with talons for nails

Penanggalan

Area: Malay Peninsula

Features: Just a head with entrails and long hair hanging from it; fangs and an invisible tongue; smells of vinegar

Rokurokubi

Area: Japan

Features: Head that leaves the body on an extremely long neck; face of a human by day, face of an ogre by night

Strigoi

Area: Romania

Features: Pale skin; hollow, red-rimmed eyes; bony hands with broken fingernails; decayed clothing from being buried underground; some can take the form of cats, dogs, or sheep; two hearts

Vlad Dracul

Area: Transylvania, Wallachia

Features: Mustache; long, dark hair; fine clothing

Vrykolakas

Area: Greece

Features: Reddish complexion; bloated bodies; roams during the day and at night

Glossary

anesthetic: something, usually medicine, that causes a person to lose feeling or awareness

apparition: ghost

demonic: like a demon

enhance: improve

entrails: the organs and parts inside a person's body

entwine: to twist together

frenzy: wild activity

garment: clothing

gnarled: full of knots, twisted

grisly: horrible, gross

gruesome: awful

heighten: to make greater

mimic: to copy what another person looks or sounds like

nomadic: not settling in one place

paralyzed: not able to move

sinister: frightening

tantrum: an outburst of anger or disappointment

tousled: messy

unquenchable: a thirst unable to be satisfied

vicious: doing mean things

vulnerable: able to be hurt

wizened: wrinkled because of age

For More Information

Books

Gee, Joshua. *Encyclopedia Horrifica: The Terrifying Truth about Vampires, Ghosts, Monsters and More.* New York: Scholastic Inc., 2007.

Kopp, Megan. *Real-life Vampires.* Mankato, MN: Capstone Press, 2011.

Pipe, Jim. *Vampires.* New York: Bearport Publishing, 2007.

Vorgard, Treval and Lisa Trumbauer. *A Practical Guide to Vampires.* Renton, WA: Wizards of the Coast, 2009.

Woog, Adam. *Vampires in the Movies.* San Diego, CA: ReferencePoint Press, Inc., 2011.

Web Sites

Chupacabra
animal.discovery.com/tv/lost-tapes/chupacabra/
Find out about Chupacabra sightings and other creatures.

Dracula: Fact and Fiction
www.history.com/videos/dracula-fact-and-fiction#vampire-myths
Watch videos about the history of vampire myths, Count Dracula, and Vlad Dracul.

Haunted Charleston
www.mycharleston.us/gullah.html
Learn more about the Boo Hag and other legends of Charleston, South Carolina.

Vlad Dracula
www.middle-ages.org.uk/vlad-dracula.htm
Learn more about the man who helped inspire Dracula.

Index